HARVEST LINGO

Also by Lionel Fogarty

Kargun
Yoogum Yoogum
Kudjela
Ngutji
Jagera
New and Selected Poems: Munaldjali, Mutuerjaraera
Minyung Woolah Binnung: What Saying Says
Yerrabilela Jimbelung: Poems about Friends and Family
Connection Requital
Mogwie-Idan: Stories of the Land
Eelahroo (Long Ago) Nyah (Looking) Möbö-Möbö (Future)
Selected Poems 1980–2017

LIONEL FOGARTY

HARVEST LINGO

NEW POEMS

First published 2022
from the Writing and Society Research Centre
at Western Sydney University
by the Giramondo Publishing Company
PO Box 752
Artarmon NSW 1570 Australia
www.giramondopublishing.com

Cover and design by Jenny Grigg
Typesetting by Andrew Davies
in 9/15 pt Tiempos Regular

Printed and bound by Pegasus Media & Logistics
Distributed in Australia by NewSouth Books

A catalogue record for this
book is available from the
National Library of Australia.

ISBN: 978-1-925336-17-7

9 8 7 6 5 4 3 2

The Giramondo Publishing Company acknowledges the support
of Western Sydney University in the implementation of its book
publishing program.

This project has been assisted by the Commonwealth Government
through the Australia Council, its arts funding and advisory body.

I dedicate this book to revolutionary Aborigines
up-and-coming new writers
and worldwide Indigenous writers

Contents

Section One

Section Two: India Poems

Section Three

Section Four

Section One

Intruder Wants the Writer

To write as a child to be a man
No boxes of childhood voice
my present, writing details.
No hidden child backward growing up
gains my learned on the road sky.
Future's song dance lit pen friends for me in evenings
Not one sort of personal fireworks voice,
gave rise to the now existence dared.
Reluctance response by these ages,
Spare me not remorseful teenage pandemonium.
Pare her tempest defiant with red yellow brown ochre.
Breathe well inside the walls of rooms helplessly undecided.
No baby's cries touch my raiment saddest crutch lost of mum's death.
Those life survivals by childhood happenings are snapped
by swine trample readership.
Embellishing more than needed.

Hands Bleeding

After life, after future lives.
The poetry massacred my tears of sad brim into happiness.
The poet knew tightened hearts kill the innocence.
The writer's law fell as the protest poet listens to nobody
    No voice No fights
But for all the politics of parents.
We became past assembled now truth
before tomorrow tender sharp all those selves as payrolled moments.
Sway recognised fires lay for glorified walkabout
as if it's time to mind
write natural write
while the wind bakes the delicate floods.
For every post in the grounds of a Black man's, Woman's lands,
Costly costs must pay.
Massacre the thought of murderers
Be a Poet: Fucken Hard Work.

Yo I Am the Man

Who gave you woman
don't know who us is ha ha
Voice the name black babe
Not our son, not our daughters
Yo who your name means
What voice gives sound to the works of a poet
Yo who your word name gave to the creative performers.
Hey voices of no meaning singling on voice over
box stand-over makes no unity;
Pure voice, pure poets.
Your name voice-man made no childrens' art word
life-long stories.
Where the name spun by White man name up
a black man using the name for message.
What gave the name rights man right to rewrite history
by giving change to the land names?
Cities name made us blame
Identity lives on names by culture, rename the voice
    enmity by a lie's call.

Constructive Gratitude

Imagination buggered up a nation
He man buried structured thoughts
by wandering freedom's mystery.
Memory bangs back and forward
in the measure sparks balmy
cold evening as tucked away
companions sustain a magnet
    passion's remnants.
Imagination no poor disruption
When the monsoon gave loud hypotheses
to these hate force emotions.
Imaginative rich husband falling in love
with the poor men's wives,
Just as justice fire-generated inflicts depth
of sorry we done intensity to your cities.
Convey all relevant extremisms for terrorism
happen to be socially supple by acquired haunt grudgingly
Army ingenuity empathetic.
Imagination of no languages

Organs Purities Nature Blood

Nah don't test your blood for those money-making doctors;
Nurse nurse your purses.
Defect the expense foods the method newly carriage blood justices
When ate in then mature answers.
No health care risk by the system cause disorderly.
Sperm the brain's bodies free as genetics must not pay.
Painful are the childbirths bringing rich blood aflow.
Beverages are parties' pressure for blood to behave consumery
inappropriately renders empty rich stomachs.
The world temptative over and over people's lung failures and
    poisoned membranes;
Nah don't give blood for tests injustices cause most are poor to afford.
Let bloods run free as rivers an seas.

Deprivation

Hysteria embers of rippling aftermath
came in the bliss of my lovers
embraced racked satiated
gaze by the dark spoken
screams as she fathom our licked
momentum impacted psyche
Quick melody melting happy visible signs gave us complexion.
The glory of determination lasting a century
unravels young man's face tousled a complete silence.
But slender the eyelashes chiselled names in clouds.
This inquisitive eerie reverberative whispered molten glimmering years
over years made arched brows yawn into the dawn.
Now dilapidated tongues question, ring thousand hysteria
breakfast for lovers bliss to never refresh death

Solutions a Combine

Legacy me the poor to poet's post
Lend us the hands not written
Leg those bodies can't move bikies.
Foul mouth on floor trying to speak while travellers listened
to proofread luxurious cockroaches.
A glamorous goose hair stood communicating with the woman
men that ignored lovers consistently change games.
Beyond the legacy of newly built homes,
gave pursuit to the people in suits.
Transform compromise now of legacy, the office delivers.

Annual Pottery Travel Floods Brochures

At risk resilience reduce offending
At principles implements well resounded
Oh yea shambles of man degraded consideration
Oh no shambles of solitude decayed by activity
Oblivious commodity came eternal when pathetic
Disasters were given vanish reticulation
We rather perish earth oppressors
We better shape sickness to be outwitted
Idealised deliver divorced ghostly petrified
Sensual hanger-ons still outshining
The narrowed seldom daring senseless
Fight in prone in trench token devour
Faces were custom pity prudence
The noisy silly poetry turn as politics
Smiles made deafness, hear lively minds
Then unshadowed disturbers mutilated
Intense moaned museums
Then programmed nerve field masters
As if manicuring betrayal renunciation
Rush inquisitors test tongues near beheaded
Plunder as flesh first cheats lay
Robed in lyric pure evenings.
Those silencing pale mist around names
Catalogued a contract forfending
Glory freeing spiteful.
Now shadows burnt between years
Past life recalled Australians.

Sterility brag menace offensive
For our compulsive blatant enhancement
Not Jillaroo an Cocky be exploit their wise answers,
Will never never cease.
Link together willingness all strangest blood crap;
Not prepared for ancient modern
Rattles to show sign, in unshambles says.
Motherhood as apprenticeship.

Amour Lionel's Love Poem

AMOUR OGINAL'S DES POET CAMPS SONT MON AMOUR
AMOUR EST MA LEXE
SERUBOSUET ACHES PANS IAMOUR DE BROUSSE
ET NOUS DISOUS
L'AAOUA EST IENGE
Amour est vivante et recu
Amour est un kangaroo
Amour est un emeu
Amour est iamour de la vein
Amour est me ami
Et nous
qui n'ons pas d'amour?
Amour est la terre
Eh bien, l'amour sons,
Nous MURRI savons
C'est L'Amour mal aimee
Donnon nousice lámour. DONNEA BÁMOUR
Notre Dreamtming, est amour
Attrape mon d'amour
la eu diamour
La culture est notre amour
La culture est nous memes dans l'amour
L'école ne donnes pas d'amour

Alors Nous Black Power nous vous donnons l'amour
Fieret simple...ement
L'amour est l'amour
a nos terre d'amour
AMOUR MARCH AVEC MOI
AMOUR REVEILLE TOI AVEC MOI
Maintentant donnen nous la amour veritable

'Under Over the Rainbows'

It's fair we have charcoal colours people
    Being black child skinned by past.
It's fair we have European cloth
        But our art black not lacked.
We have darkest blue-eyed baby
      White with complexion from a dark race.
It's fair physically to keep love in own
     Race speaking singing English or not.
We may material all things white parentheses.
    Yea but caste is half fullest to all human mentally black people.
They mightn't mine old bludger sex anymore, the naked began to swim.
Bones blooded addicted spirit gave fair care a drug voice so alcoholic.
Better being of black sky light morning night never being palmed by lies.
Moon sliver peace just us now,
Sun redden please just us now,
Stars umbilical scalpel surgical the sterilised.
Wind dwellers purest those selectivity,
Specimens blanket enlighten burden of those rich unwittingly on arrival.
Its first race wills keepers to the lasting are not seen touched or spoke
        on toiled.
It's benediction of Father Mothers smoke fire cherish sweetness
        symmetrical on our souls campfire said wrote now painted.
Precision your blackfellas now babes
The race of your birth did know colour.
It's fair when we black people off the charcoal not mined

New Year Birth

Wanna crazy new year
Wanna sweet six fair din coming's
Temple the land fights by
Our black dancers and painting the story to
Live lifes...
Want to thieves no back return,
For they still wanna thieves our lands;
Big man stays on love's silent wave
On the day land changed.
Who gave manse's want to too
Speakers pave mint tongues.
We mother unbait controls
Who gave the knowhow.
Cooking fire for raw
Dry leaves;
Eyes show the ear giveth
By the want to the born
Again freedom library

A Poet a Day, a Suicide a Week

Defiant sad landscape
Where's the lavish coat of born essentials?
Enter a world were lavish quest
Can't speak their harvest lingo
Religious, flor cool fauna
Stocks the gold stolen
Poets take lies pains away
Gold got took did not make good luck
Where no spend papers kill trees roots

Time's Out of Balance

Half wrote in the inch of futures
Inch me along relations
I never meet my death by theft,
How many histories inches the hands that hold a voice to reward those
 not heard.
Well so few rode vehicles by not chasing bumper bars, as the driver lost
 his way, just to be payed more.
Years ago I did not want to go to these places, inch of earth allotted
Nails hammered into my tongues when dreaming season
all came the morning sun night days.
Blood flowed fast to my brain, just then cuts flashed ray shot red eyes
 open the sky rainbows ears to listen, as babies went to sleep, by
 the Mothers and Fathers wind washing sound of new communities
 rushing sign to never give into hells

Modern Canvas Boats Comfort Who Cares

Poets take lies pain away
Poor and inbetween poor are living painters
This world is not homeland
The earth is a homeland
Homeland home house home trans
Must heart, but a house as a cave
Written lips are wisp from what's read in to books.
Seasons are the timeless fields
Set them to write speak sing the struggles,
but to gain justice with the rice wind hail stars morning first sun lights.
This world guts rich peoples to their gutter fears.
The earth smiles for flowers are the plant by small people's big loves.
DHANYAVAAD;
Sing on every share 'DHANYAVAAD'
Heal no more pain healing to futures foods that market
where no spend papers kill trees roots.

Section Two: India Poems

Ideal Crowded Streets

Streets are born, streets are life.
Streets are careful deserted streets in early mornings
loom from nights constant change.
Success serves those sold by crew
Demolished building impressive low classes where arts in streets
are taken away, for new leaves old scenes by the living.
Neighbourhoods part the bare drawn city;
Bones elegant offer cheap wearings.
Many untouchable escape back into favourite abandoneds.
How long decades take to page pieces of concrete fencing
will storefront the village street wealth.
Architecture are the alley offers ways,
Towers fallen but erected brews in tents canvases
safe booms all beautiful smiles delighted.
Truck full of people riding hot spots to re-owned dreams.
popular train homes as cuisines hid in teams.
More fare on wheel meals deals
tomorrow now no deserted streets.

Dalit Lets Fees Histories

Australians main
Collective western suttee
for Aboriginal languages to be study:
But none taken study, harm just speaks written
In English at your home houses.
School full stop in workshop month
Abo's Black Fiery Aus Lingo.
1. Sharing policy
2. Publishing commons
4. Connection grassroots unpublished works
5. How to get national underdogs intertwine pashed
Coffee pays fees, tea rewriting histories
Lit area coming century
Dalit must light the writers
Where multilingual arise powers must
Not mix tongue twist tongues
    I use to write
    Now I fight for rights
I use to paint
    Now I'm plane lightings
I use to speak
    Now I seep tongues untied
I use to want fistfuls plantroom
    Now used your desk on mountain
Below dirt water for mud.......

She was on the ways to Amerika jealousy WARU HER MOONS,
MULTI CULTURES COLLABORATED BY JUSTICES IMPROVED
YET CREATOR
MAPS BECAME 2050 TO 2030S COUNTRY WITHOUT.
SHE ICINGS ENTICING THEY INTERNATIONAL palay DHA palay before
They said who cause advance anthology teams for her now
Say those numbers more histories to the left overs...

Benefits are Made By the Poor Affordable

50 TO 20 YEAR WHAT CUTS DELHI POOR TO ARDOUR
Every street felt sad, but dated glad
Hi every street is a fire glass by dires
fry hearts best beat kind beauty even blind.
Every street is homeless
Every street is a need
Every street pisses a man crave
Small soil smell the sip oil
gas into lands not registered.
Small animals press sunshine down light
for there cows are scared roam by milk honey path
feets to the fields of farmers daughters
wanting men's rich bodies strong.
High, low, streets moistures sweat powerful
draining to the bosses' household.
Purse lust now the poor pocket.
They caught greater sleep on every corner where
earth paved wave, for new creative brick stove
    lifers cookers street.

Symbiotic Inter Affirmation

Timid admiration came over me for the tarnished sensation of their
great bashfulness homes.
It didn't worried being rich at this abandon of poor triangle.
It did not bristled me to dislike the rich person around festivals
enamoured amples,
Fat daughters exposured music poetry till an emulated performer
gave chastity
a world of it's own abundant.
Temperamental creative poet's reform powers into improvisation
literature.
We sang blossomed selfish suppression by dragging jailed
men to the final blow.
Ocean ray sun redecked all skins on man's married consumed looks.
But timid in an empire I assigned a ragged love for rich disturbance
made me sensation more rich people my snippets.

Jaipur Airport Colour Wear World's Apart

In other world away the streets are burning fire for cooking living
sleeping and using nature's calls.
Just them show, no any justice given
In another dark man's cities, where lands are lined by small shops.
Cars are slower on the move
People's feet move fast in timeless spaces giving rest to all wants of works.
These roads passages a new age as the poor struggle a door into lifes bright eyes.
Many Gods seek the spirits of begging emotion just to flower the heat wave over pollution's reins.
Many a houses tent those staying almighty to write.
Sad tears can't be drops for the blood rush in all humans to do positive walks to talk together,
even share rains disappearing pain

The Poor are Well Organised Than the Up-Class

Common memory of all fights for every suns to reach the blind
Common feeling sees all love's not weight on the feature futures
Common soul all are holders of and in keepers to tomorrow
people unite now to unity gives
    strength to up an coming writer.
('POETS ARE ALL THERE TOO')
Summer stream the cold before ages growth
Summer seem more faint of charm swayed winds
Strange summer open an immaterial emotion, when precious
Significant village where feed miracled fresh branches
Romance rain fell on the roofs for all refinement
Here the recipient strains fuse looks, by those sad close up houses.
Romantic science stopped for our natural smiles
Taste food on the streets as no vague smells by the dawn ponds
        swimming fishes.
Mute ate down by the tree that fell for fire logs the rich people's needs.
Me softly presence frame in a lapse as my mind ahead breezes not mine
Found silvery endless whispers saying 'your home ours, our home yours'.
Symbols by arts are letters in all approaches
The night fell under the ground door ways to a days bright image taken
        by dancers.
Sing the temples back to bush silence where mysteries will never
        be casements
A poet moves people, changes society, not white man laws.
Aflame common men's on every levels
Do save lakes rivers seas for future, won't have any trailing.
Artists know when the heat tint the skin

Artists know when the stories are cold even when hot
Surrender the outer-space sacrifice
Most are meaningless by an eye's dim lantern
Common rights don't needs to fight
Common books are read over+over
Till those who can not write will write their own way
Common soul will never let sinking boat taken over
Tomorrow children leave tales behind and share common songs
makes the old to be your young;
Relation heard, don't be lost forgotten

Can't Speak Their Harvest Lingo

Religious flora cool fauna
Angels breeze adventurous literature
KOLKATA = CALCUTTA, TREK ALL WORDS.
Till the cows come home
KALI cuttin dem duty silk
smooth men's heads around necks that turn on her looks.
Please alliance the stars for our achievements.
Gods musical beaches as industry partners landmarks ceremony.
To eligible a destination at highest satisfaction
gave route goals for a confirm writers return.
Those of history are colosseum in nonstop experience entertainment.
Foreigners clipping their interior to institute
to come over our first people's nation gratitude Aus Oz
Warehouse of ages make the nationalities entrance.
Bid for digestive emergetic spirit
Yo balance life elements scrambles properties for all paths not diseased
Kolkata January cold excited my soul meriting candle lit romantic

Sense of Elation, Tranquility

All land sea sky universal
Scatter our matters to all masters
Ascend fragrance hopes in acceptance
immense enjoy workers appreciation.
Thousand sightings are keeped to the anthem of the struggle.
Heal not an ardent where no one listens.
Logs walk the ants singing melody
Sweet fully got agony soft on the lips thirsting for flagon of wine.
Moths that gave death to the butterfly assembled mankind.
All ground breeze into tender growth giving inspiration to those who been immolated.
Settler burnt dusty brown terrified acquaintance
Come unbaked thousand years bread ate in provinces.
Ascend us the affective traveller,
twinkle and invading all observance.

No Fame to Snoring Roars

Problems gutter sleep
Trees fall, houses have dead halls
Send us your wise soul voice to the pillow
of brain's minds' airways resting.
Separation hurt loneliness clutched people moments of war.
Natives up to date accomplishments.
Send classes gnostic spiritual pillows heads tidying the hymn
School not those who don't want to eager learning actions.
Totally the service lives of propriety point flood of restless anger.
Yet distance's vestry chases demons away from responsibilities
Music speaks under sheets of medically fortunate kiss.
There are the elaborating anniversary pretty toned up refreshing
    government parents.
Oh well ask of last sleeping noticed coincidence bed time
repertoire snores writers score harden pillows.
Problems are gutter sleeps

All Markets are All Universes

Universal not own by anybody
Universal food must not be own, by anyone
Universal water must not be owned, by anybody
Trees are reef thirst of every hearts pulse beat
Channels of all first nation got to be relations
Changing all first people, to be what they want won't do;
The cycle of life, all survive by truth quenched by justices.
'Poor will be shops of their own'
The bikes cars bus trams all types are everyone's travel,
When planes fall remember who flyed first without steels.
There is honey in every worlds, don't sip its poisons
Marriage those loves before the communicate.
Many adorable smeared words came from the wrong TV internets
Many agony are fibs by the society, who think they closing us better ha ha
The heart on legs knee the hair of all air
    sound mad, but man made by land has a chance.
Lots of mornings desire joy the sad which nests
Lots stabbed by the top nut on the wheels fast
    slow as if peace is the dark blood moneys.
Remove the worn out old times
Remain our supreme before new world order came
Relive the paradise where the finger are the painters
    maps to the earth unhurt.
Cultures of we native no matter where we are in this worldliness, are
        to come back
Struggled by battle as to help by are the healed kind vein the good lay by
        sick human

being trying to be us as anybody.

The drain of the sewage sometime bring more life in escaping a cage up
    cell sleeps

Firewood is wealth beyond the stove planner cooked matchmakers.

Landloves are not a city path road only when earth has the right to awaken
    the babies bornunborn.

Universal Fathers an Mothers send all us the owner of hearts life-fulls.

All the markets are all universes

Stay Alive Next 16 Years (Fish Trap)

The poor must gain all what rich desire
'That day comes that night will come'
Desire for justice every morning
    Heal all lonely poor every night
Decry the sky tears to no more suffering
Delight the faces of earth smile
where rivers meet the sea
the cities are made on soils
birth by nature's fire desires
Most desires are met by rainbows
Little life needs full beauty as showing a growth of lives
Just us we pour love as laws.
    But the practice works injustice,
Cause rich class, wants are always
    in needs of the poor to stay;
cold hot cold leaving never old Hey the rich know not music,
cos the poor has justice's music
Desire high days buys futures at costs
    of lent humans.
Desire low makes the car pathways
pick up broken heart on bikes
rode down crown streets.
The worlds are wounds help by pollution
Let the space be not wiped, bring the air clean
pure water free for all those that pay for it now.
Sounds of earth best must still be holding
    us in cities together no matter who citys on any countrys.

All desire just to be real for healthy bodies
make the sex of love stop wars by injustice men's.
More desire for the Mother, Father spirits
of good over bad, gives hearts bloods,
one on one for the desire to fight the struggles of any
to be better with a funeral to evils forever.
No tree desire lips mouth truth
Let justice be peace by walking awaken
    closed eyes closed ear.
We don't want desire to be dead leaves.

Section Three

'Aloha For Aotearoa'

Maui.......may have met Ngunda fishing once,
I once didn't like the Maori native [I don't know]
for what some of them done to we,
brothers at the path of a pub.
There was four of them hit tings and kicking
into my Brothers bodies and heads cosh
they had a disagreement of a racial think.
The Murri said you don't come
from here piss off over your place.
They swear at each other bad.
This was in the year 1974 and it still
going on in this year.
But after understanding the Maori native
at bush where we worked as ringbarking.
I said to one of them you brown people hey;
And they all jump up and said
we are black people and Aboriginal like you.
Well why don't you go over there and help the one's
who are fighting for land and keep their culture alive
The Maori turned and said well how would you know
of us if you didn't meet us Hey.
Yea Sisters and Brothers of New Zealand
We just found out that name is a white name for your country.
And us here must respect your land as 'Aotearoa'
Maori   I'm with you in spirit we are with you in love unity.
Our cultures are similar maybe.
We believe in the Creator as Mother and Father

and above Beiami came and gave as life
and mother earth born us as children to look after her.
Oh Maori people my eyes cry when our people are lost
unfounded tribes mixed tribes gone and culture helped
by old cause of fear to tell the young
for they will abuse in white man's ways.
The sunrise of Maori ancient culture now seems to me unity and shared.
I have learned you Maoris have a treaty signed long ago, together with,
Pakehas miggloos or moy moy we say they ghosts.
Anyway them whites didn't honour the treaty today,
will some be given and over here some is given
but whites still fly around like blowflies to bite our land
In the begin we fought with spears and many weapons but were taken over,
lots of us die like people die,
but we lived, survived and kept most of our culture going.
Now we teach in family to respect our tribal ways.
But most of us drink the evils of society tasted wines beer yes,
my Murri people are washed in the sins of white people's values.
Of course all natives were affected by the blood buried by a past
Maori you are our brothers and sisters of future to come
as one to give freedom to all who suffered.
They say we voyage here to Australia
but we believe we came from the land sprang from our gods
danced sang and hunted here in beginning of time.
The coming of the Maori is the coming of a great race,
we all you are the first there and will remain there forever.
Now Captain William Hobson was a man who deliberately fooled
or used the signing of the Treaty to take the land
anyway I reckon he had no choice.
You Maoris would have wiped them Pakehas out

and ancestor proud and ready for war but was peaceful like us.
Anyway 1840 is no different to now.
Traditional accounts are remembered in native, for it's our pride,
like you are proud of the canoe that took you on voyages.
I been told Maori went everywhere in the world,
well you must come here to once in our lifetime.
The story of Takitimu must reflect the big migration of all Polynesians
Oh excuse me if I'm wrong, but your god,
Kahukura is a form of a rainbow led the way to Aotearoa,
well we sailed in the canoe of life.
Sure me don't know much of your culture
but we are all part of the sky, stars and animals, sea and land.
So Maori brothers, you are warriors even today,
well come over here and kill a few whites Ha Ha
We in Australia are native who ask anyone 'Where are you from?'
not like whites 'who are you'.
Across the sea you are and we are but we will be together
in sternness and respectful love for all native,
We got together more often so there's no misunderstanding.
We will link your Aloha with our love
in a lifestyle where we all love happy on earth.
The changes by the demands of modem society
can't stop our spirits unifications,
The spirituality of murri is in attitudes to nature, like you yes,
I haven't been on your land but I feel with you
in cultural unity and to keep all our good old ways going Maori people,
I love your singing in lingo and feel it has touched my heart.
Earth magic is here with all natives.
We have carving and weaving strictly mainland to our ritual
ceremonial culture

of cause most of our murri people are down where whites settle, so we
have lost a lot
but keep a bits and these are the bits we share with you all.
The sun is the same to all natives.
The supernatural is forever in all us natives.
Our relationship with nature is in our daily life.
With spiritual natives we will give life a better future for our children.
We must dance the war dance against the evil of man
and destroy it with spiritual loves.
In 1769 that white James Cook
You Maori should have speared him
anyway them other natives done it.
But now knowing the treaty of Waitangi was sign gives you power
to fight the Pakehas on legal ground.
As for us Abos we didn't even have a sit down and talk but was fired on
at sight.
Oh yea, they say there's this treaty by Batman in Victoria
for tea, tobacco and blanket,
Well lucky we didn't all sign a Treaty cos all paper signed
wrote by white man lies and never respects and poisons all history.
But now white man here want a give us paper for land
and not take word of mouth for granted or truth.
You had the 'fire in the fern' during 1863 to 1872
well we tried burning their houses and killing sheep cattle and even
staged a warfare
as I have read one Maori sang out to the British at Orakau
'we will fight on forever, forever'
And you are still fighting.
Hey Maoris
The Bay of Plenty was a conflict too

And I have heard of a massacre for four years and withdrew defeated at
King Country.
Yes I see we all fight for our rights.
And racist people are still keeping that thing we are savages and not
worthy of life.
They took our land but took our singing spirits for our children's.
Yes Maori people you are your own race,
but remember we over here are black like Maori........
Oh yes colour of skin is not matter to our cultures.
One brief flaring moment I wish I was over there with you going the Haka
Once my attitudes were I don't like Maoris, now I'm wait in
to arisen in the same sun and sleep under the starring night
or lay in the rain with our faces same amid wimp in your rivers, seas of life,
Sure I'm an Abos in Australia,
But Maori brother and sister are native wise bright
and the gods watch over us,
Murri and Maoris

1972 Plucked From My Eyes

Still in high school but about ten jumped
the train to see the big smoke city for my peoples
families were staying there
cause they want a more freedom
to work and socialise with other(s) the same.
The hills were covered by a green not smelled by the nose these days.
The creek were a smell off the sea air
a breeze as if fish were big but small
when town reach the city.
Tree were happy smile show on faces
until city town funny tree replanted
By a differ earth sway rooted
mantises man made goanna be a dam over that river.
So the old said *'fish here they'll get rids this big river soon'.*
The sun was ever meeting night day in lights brighten
by the fire made by chip off green wooded barks fallen
With these happening not good food
made thoughts bad
made gut hungry.
With these change came time –
less of important like season cold and the hot
took many children's mums and dads to sweat for some other
family's futures.

Koala Tress Turn Her Borobi

She was pretty young Borobi being put in the tree by her human Father
for 4 hours,
As he walk back to the other Jarjum, they ask 'Where's Borobi?'
he said 'Oh she jump into a tree wanting to eat leafs and looked happy
so I let her be what she wanted to be, a Borobi.'

Many Bilin Bilin (king parrot) flirted around flying high and low seems
like listen to old Kargaru (kookaburra) sing a song to have a birth.
While on the lily pads waters the Taran (frog) was loud yell help in
crooker ways.
But the Nyunga Nyunga (bower bird) was signing a dance so to attract
Wogun Wogun (scrub turkey) to give tosh tongue to the air of life
that was in tree.
But young Borobi kept on moving from tree to branches being a Queen of
the top.
This time doped up she fell out of the tree, just in time for her dad Binga
to catch her, hold her in his arms, say she be alright and will
sleep tonight.
That young Borobi found her pretty face changed.
She sang 'they are my people the birds animal around I loved the
4 hours forever'.
Borobi had many Jarjums after this the tree got bigger than all her friends.
Now the story is never go into a tree for a long time cause you can
be missed.

Al Qaeda Means the Word of God
(The Word of God Sometimes Means Dog)

Multinational democracy
  loyal to convenience
        loves barriers.
Multinational halo
a hippie
    free market machinery.
Bigotry in the corporate
Fascism is the dead flower for every dead
    voice
Terrorism is not sovereignty breeding
Disillusionment labelled by those as truth wrote
uncivil non-resistance gave mindless spiritless register.

Privatised cruise missiles mistaken
plundered natural resources for them war alliance.
Intrinsically evil edifices heaven
greedy bankers elected and kept to the possibly last drop...
Bombs are made from pragmatism
in long an short cheating un-monitored authorities.
Propaganda quasi-bugging embedded journalists Superpowers' will self-
        destructive because human will channelises
the down fall of amorphous supremacy
Imperial archive gives amplified paranoia
pre-emptive hell Mandate history, qualify invasion as a world occupation
    poor are starved = provocative
The word of God sometimes means dog

A Mementos Verse to Young Tips For Tacks

Young people never die, their dead are waters we drink
Silence crevasses wash and dry ochred by keepers
Young people must not be babe people
    When stories are told to uphold.
The earth is responsible for more than life
The world hangs on pictures farmed
By attributing wise words that came from
Burning fires embed by smoke fireflies
In eyes to ears not seen.
Young people became old only at the true
    Camp to camp mobs can speak dance evening sun night
With everything in foresight.
Bewilder signpost made we swear
Being wild in the alien feelings matter
The past to futures sleepily tucking society direct
familiar conservative winds memories
refresh soul blowing gave all homelands piles of whisper
Songs sang are never lost as if when it begun.
Mirages vein dust devil Gnarl Rivers
Chants the last stand when the young men sat down first to stand.
Retaliate hate to be muddled so alert the extend kind
opted topic to be in relation over crimes sniping steams.
Soft lugged small people's enthusiasm are shadow voices, for better,
        for healthier.
    Young peoples never dead their dead are waters we drinking now hey?

A First Note About the Regions

I opened the door that
Morning to the horror of society
Sis we got to pay another 250
To get our brother's coffin to the church
We already given all we got

Section Four

Moody Mr Modi

Get up be awake wages by 2 cent
Make him spend a cent to rent.
His Dad made tea now he tease
Who give a share bed how your pillow sank to poems
of neo flashed lie in written story hey man.
The made did not make us made it's just use where came from;
changed nothing at the body of it halls.
Bring down a prize for high prices
His wife had better life no harms in who word the alarms.
Wife die more lifes.
Terror run the laws still kept by whites mens in bed
finding there mother son's cry of slave minds slaved souls.
Stop region wars by a day of seeing both sides of the words
world pictures in the eyes of youth that tea the jobs for 2 cents.

Jammine Projects

Money have honey money
the gold stock stolen
the steel stock stolen
Double the reserve debt back so the Government friend
can purchase by small prices.
The sellers were the real land owners,
under ground rights are lights.
Crisis came expensive
Gold got took, did not make good luck.

Vendors reach out in rush times,
Can’t multiplex a cold peoples
Can’t curate an old peoples

await the rainbows golden feets
at the end of poor pedestrians.

Man Monocultures Silly

Man monocultures silly under capitalism

Monocultures monetary arise death
as they lumps \
many temporary
insane blind desires.
I can imagine fuss away
I can imagine positivity aways
Dreaming anatomy biology chemistry
cultures maimed society.
Share shelter comfort, not awards.
Real threats,
Those passionate hates, are hard.

Must fragrance troubled smells;
Untrue loves shames.

Manmade monos are a detriment to change,
all yearning for the starry sublime express.

Pour the mind which were behind.
Never rush a wall closer with sureness
As hearts in bodies need
blood lines, songs.

Monoculture is no culture when no
dances song painting conjures
Monoculture no cultures

Accept the Queen's Lovers

Death wish truths
Corruption by PMs warps reality
Corruption buying Knight's honour by night
He look so listed on a keen monarchist clock back outgrown
    colonial medal,
Money forkship by the tax well=spring bankers, public mindset workers.
The root 62 open mature years debate ties closer on a shorten
re-pus drank in training.
Young making mistakes
Our 62 years frame bodies were rape of inspiration
OK let them have Queen's patron favour now republicans highest
break away first reign.
Makes a differ mates of ships
The order of Australia lies dishonest list a lot in opposition
No royals are corruptive
but the governments use of votes prove times are behind.
The great graffiti not their country but they have a society;
Awards for the warps of surprise.

Bunch of Hookers Needs Looks

As requite hearts, those recommence pulse bloods
As reminisce green glue blue lips smile sponsored
grateful interaction ideas various loves
swim walk even look tormented
Perfect stun, perfect hugs gowns gorgeous as mooring
celebrate for future times.
Competition mothers; voiceless fathers
Accessible tolerance was offenders regular please unjust ice
for those signed witness harvest break-in.
Exception bars afar out, passing even prints
Safer flourishing feels are thoughts to requite unsolved
Crisis gratefully glues.
Accused by all delusional rorting hearts made all charges seem rant
and chosen by opposition trenchant trails by witness not heard or seen.
Mocking gags as notions came motion
saga on spent time lives not of national transparency.
Our majority debate victims the peoples up growth,
just so bastardry rich can play off the
poor lines ignorant mens' public reputations.
Conspiracy by money innocence grates the safe saving
we don't want gallery paint or pain to be receiving hate
process in the due of the next mornings.
Lynch counted courts are many numbers.
Laboratory truth must requite all hearts knows feels no policies.
Bunch of hookers needs looks.

Aug 21 22 2011

Farewell to those coconuts commissioned to the
2 Stronger Futures governments.
So appointed sleeks
confident future on seconds chance
or plot plans government.
never flowers those hand outs.

New barbarian Territory laws
Top End made down under
White still reserved
to operate the
Black first
Pursued education

Black red golden rainbows to be milk bar
Museums

Pose Non War Prime Mr

Bring back our army
Corporations are motiving war beyond our knowings.
Remove every state in the world, for communities has the powers.
Stop conflicts, don't go over there, not your society.
Suspend (Evict) the evil of your own Suspend (Evict) the devils of your
White politic,
Government cops in homelands where criticism rains like a thousand
guns cannot

Bring back our army no matter where are the emerged.
Time now to issue a warning, what's really inhumane?
Come home give
up, give down.

Happy Tears Dams the Sad

Merry in your hometown

Merry tomorrow in your hometown

Merry the fires feathered by birds
Flying justice onto mountains
Magic is the land untouched
Respects yams seeds as
Stars up sews....

Back Man Lingers 2020–30s

72 per cents cents on 59 per chances
Come back critical felted keys
To anti-activists 'shows us a Abos ministers first black
Austrians for all poor be ideology savers
To wholes intervention off or of love non politics
Works in aspiration element programs
'Government, in come managements worked'
Never administered infrastructure with
auditor general climate remoteness
or modem's unequivocally essential
Abruptly suffer in vote's agenda unknown

Smell evidence, touch evidence Insist evidence strategic bold
the children's
emboldened wages so taxed tax and tax
Quarantine those who still attend school
land school home school pays fees
Evaluation 16 communities COM=measures
under instances believed safer was always the starts of
unhealthier policys, now expensive
implementatives costs main similar politics,
nothing for nothing brings nothing
Privately thesis consultants say
from tops classes to bottom constitution
don't due or over recognition clauses,
panel accurately, only if referendum gives righties or mistakes
To Anti constitution were to discriminatory

when heard what people who people's
Pets pet's advisory would end Mothers suffering, Fathers suffering
children's states
Repeating validated mistakes of the past
stronger futures tax an tax improves

Bosses Bud Turbulent Consul

Consul rock never removed
Consul shop removed to the never never
Consul loom deliver of an ignoble future,
Revenge not the venges given on broken
    Shell faces swirling.
Scraped astounded ground among vines
Were a thousand tapestry backbones?
Lived even shield by the oldest,
Spear the dust in a shrine where it fragile
Anger into crust offerings.
Feeble rusty illusive merry people
are tangled in secret contentment.
Consul those who consul
    Rest perfume concrete fearsome boys and girls
in quenches by man's thirst.
Consul a lie and find loved one die.
Rest vibrant rivers in gut on feets so walk the waters,
Rest cancerous arrogant brain marks and penetrate cliffs
in alluring life's competition to be no more.
Friend exotic wander the escape migrating loves they once had.
Wrinkled in kind abandoned cloud
Yet to frolic snakes, splendours.
Consul the consulted we find embraces are arms
where freed men are obvious xenophobia.
Now consul conquest jest cheerful humankind.

Activism Sign Barter Impudent Bleedin Age Flash

Rewarding as rapid proud vibrant
Quiet library await to learn readings
Quarrel paradise centuries futures
East West commotion
South Northern continent
Year 3000 chin up, head above
    Feets feeling arms stroking
Faces moonlit skull webs sieve picks eyes
Bones lavender trekker minerals paused
Mouthing people's creek lined their bodies
Love-in regrets was dead honeycomb away
Love-in forbidden second thoughts
    Letter less legs knees as chapters
Guardian serpent parent seeing blood trees
Seeing bloodstones blood stars blood loves
Guardian serpent know to settle down
Promise choices questions given complication
    World's words earth wealth rich in hurts
Passion agreeable solved riddle souvenirs
jumble visible miniature winds
Beloved filled blanket sky covers
    Scrutinises cabin swapped league
Rewarding behaviour supplied by their
Disgusting class systems
World's words hurt earth hurled heard loves
Reprompting clumsiness laughed at mocked
Dynamite Spinifex spin baked leaves

Don’t remember stubborn heedless shingled
Furred nor primal curious
Winds tear wiped no rains body’s pains
The stay human new man
Reign merchandise luxurious scroll recrossed
Reign sophisms were innocence unconfined
Name shame inner around to be bad themes
Conformity inclination an inquisitive native
Genocide over new atrocities refuses secular
Heritage admitted colourless remnants culture
Noise matters desert smile, ghost economics
Genealogies overbanked our backs as waters
Leaf triply invaders flayed married reincarnate
Presence stab Rewards

Evocative World Classes

I hate the city when it quench
    justice love kindness as greed
        postulates wanting changes.
I hate the change congestion,
land must lust roads
    an inaugural governments' ozonezone build up sums summits

    I hate parched desperate consuming,
    mens wars over windows.
    Sworn breeze through ill clothes lines.
Eyes that checks post transferred purpose.
Possession of those interior injustice pains
that slither into fungus dark.

What hate unpacked in anger
By mimicking love's patience.
Quench instincts to believers
action spread equally.
Let self-actualisation intimidate
Injustices locality tampering
    Tenants.

Ambassador Coaches Museums;

Retiree spoken not for professings;
Exploit webs interest converse trust
Request sole reputable guest presenter
in a challenge of stereotyping scammers,
Fair emotion became victim to on life series,
Fortunate twice bedding on one community
Were quantity purchase sponsored features?
Touring motto and creeds smart customers
class impost on locality buildings became vacant.
Planning schemes seems to be remove
First succeed,
Delays inpurgative amendment
received free of charge.
Approval: *no prior use*
Permits: the trigger white mad risk
a business integrated future.
Erection cost = donation quotes
Preside fees are due;
are to be paid for by first Australians.
Invitation cake and car cause conflict to that adoption
development 'solar roads sky's'
Underway material function front walls line a defence
an apology is anticipated.
Leased applicants are provision for selected natural kits,
when gold coin is known.
Preacher dealer in parrot verses.
Expensive huge education headquartered
  recites armoured converted division.

Decolonise Medicines

Generation inquisitive Makaton
Passion luminary dramatic now
Aviation exactitude her examiner
Said for borders votes reflective
Said she gorgeous master parade,
Banquette spectacle know now.
Renaissance core accurate war
Not pro-questing inspired the accounts
Artisans' cooks.
She immune mullet breeding cycle
BUBANGAN (dolphins) await with their spears.
Those paternalisms feared diet that made
Native incorporate bay and oceans
Around diminishing protocol hunts.
He sibling even cousins sang
Decolonise consisted dances
With connection by quantity.
The DJAUWAN practice because
Elders sustain present digestion.
Generative catch them possible
Gathering into relied on
Coasted animal seasons must growth.
Passion winds hands down
Air of life winter summer
Types as PIPIS many as?

WIINYAM (mud crabs)
Luminary spending images.
The invasion exactitude middens,
    CONTINUES

Discrepancy (World Bankers)

Her hit age definition needs substantive
Transfer restitution now sub-state BANK
Repay value owner known
Recent cultural objects value high as lost
and found repatriation property.
Anthropology are ant future on road
Might highest inalienable possession
Have rights not as a conception.
Reburying skeletons are in present bodies generations
Those number of museums are but
curation
scientific true recurrence,
those rhetorics of history wrongs,

and histories Repeat

Pick front line repatriation
  Been payed, forgotten us nots
oblivion fee consigned
Patches worked into art covers.
    Spear all my ancestors
buried now to make pay.
Funnel specimens just
to dollar us undignified.
Repatriating us to rich well

off inventories is to give subsidised
powers within negotiation,
Remove from country was an administering
Money makes the repatriation go around.

Save Our Inland Seas G20

Our coast been taken again (raw hosts)
Death to the rainbow tracks (low coats)
    No more songs sunshine our legends
pathways are town roads around coasts.
Humming ancient mountains try to
    find voices of man before aspects
are promotes 'we stood on mountains'.
Thrill are still there as beginnings
  are a sacred circles
The coast inland has taken a lot,
  born land cannot be manmade.
The new city catchments are
  education on auspice to science
  and process are Shire own seas.
Sites are extremely covered by
    ongoing conflicts, dumping rubbish
Our coast crys crimes by the
  Reefs shell sea diving for
  valuable economy, parks make up lands.
A thousand bodies still
    in a linked marriage
  Permission 'save our inland seas'
Wrapped ancestors leap forward
    exposing burial burnt evidence.
  For the future children to
respect layer of family skins
Bloodline descendants are in

occupation of no haunted
living, we exchange our coast
for recorded boundaries as seas are skies.
Incursion by builders seen our sea
coast as having no say but by-the-bay riches.

YEARN RELATIVES SHARE HOLDERS

YEARS AGO YEARNING EVENING STARS
YEAR ON YEAR A YEARN WILL SEED
YEARNING LEARNED YEARS WE START.
CERTIFICATE'S CONFIRMATION AGED ABORIGINAL
NOW GIVEN TEACHERS TAX,
REVELATION IDENTITY BY SYSTEM
    MANAGEMENT;

    TARNING MEMBER WHO SELF
LITERARY CLIMATE KNOWLEDGE.

WHERE POLICY INDIG-CURIOUS
STOLEN TO BE NOT FICTION?
REVOCATION PROVIDER LETTERED TO
JOB OUR COMMUNITY
CIRCULATE POSITIONS NOT BLACK
CAN'T GET ORDERS BY THE HYPERACTIVITY
THAT'S COMPLEX 'GIVE UP'.
YEARS INTER FUTURES SHOW CULTURE
BY DANCES SONG PAINT AND CHANT
HIGHER ON WHO LAND KNOWS IT
GENEALOGY BIRTH DESCENT NOW TAKEN DNA
RORTING BLOODLINES CHALLENGE.
ROYALTIES IN FACES SCREEN THOSE SCRIBES ONCE OPEN
DECADE BELOVED NO CLAIMS.

TO BE ABORIGINAL IS RESURGENT FOREVER
RECREATIONAL TRUTH KNOWING.
YEARN ENVIRONMENTALISTS
YEAR WE WILL FACE

Alone Lips In The Seek

Missing my country and loving my homelands
Talk in to me own
Rain my heart lonely
Talk in to me own
    Pulsed my blood
Listening to other gave nothing
Being force to hear, was a pigs act.
Sitting here for the grave not to take me,
awaken in the days after made me write,
holding my body for the sex I never had,
    gave me my darkest dreams.
Letting thoughts stay on my mind gave me,
hard-lost soul of others.
Eyeing for a justice cause gave me food of needs to eat.
Hearing the word before I write made me want to art.
Speaking in past where *they* were not there,
    made me create more births.
Having men stay over gave me room to move.
Travelling weathers' lazy summers made me work.
Dry lip sip the hair on my mouth as the morning told me nights
    staring at my fears.
Birds fly by sounding loud, me to sing and not to talk.
Kangaroo jump over the sun as I leapt to catch the moon in the days.
Sad happy sad tears rushed into the streaming waters where I was to swim.
Now taken talks live by my bed and rest forever more in peace.
Talk in to me own

FACE MUMBULLA Hey Mountainy

Mumbulla was a Black Man of CASS.
Deserted brave frontline stands
Did not betray his wisdom
Our mia-mias were painted by
His hands within around our fathers.
Mumbulla is art to eyes of
Words on tip lip bedroom said
Air says death last just this life;
Big Mumbulla Big fame valley await he's smiles
Cardboard fires from left over houses newly builded
Used clever-fellers swamped down ashes dust till sundowners.
Old young Mumbullas
are still alive abate later
To fish hunt high the hills.
Those first morning fogs green covering
Country men are being flour tea sugar meeting
Sky Mumbulla so below the feet that walk the talks.
Deserted face of Mumbulla gave and gives greater art
Mapping worlds as eyes people's families to a memory
So readied;
For this happen 19.60 to 19.70's Stop awhile 2017
Mumbulla was a Black man of CASS.

For Bro Dave for Lander an any Garnet Laces Forgo.

He will always be a Brother even when not
they're for he death or in ground spoilt crimes.
Hers are fixing heritage in all ages
He's release sacred eyes happy reform.
She brought her family down to the grave
By satin he didn't make it for he's funeral,
So her drink gammon cries were soulless free to,
Your shout now, for free drugs came to his so-call sons
As if the culture back their sorrow upset over mens and womens
Who could be there at her families' beer wine tears.
Were the heart to art run-in over or down the dead which lives alive
In present just upholding soul to soul for food cheaper on the lips,
Who cares anymore.
Remember when she said he dead, she's dead and they weren't but
 just a laugh
For drink in go's and a bad joke made them coke.
Now here in real dreams to mornings after ride the sad to new daddies.
Now happy job sit bank by the fish on fish for right dishes.
for her brothers, by showing no rage over the stayed.
Fixing her heritage, she used spiritual love for dead dove birds the
 water hens.
 Burned stars' skilful lovers command a change,
 Above noise families crowned await beauty smiles
A feeling either ways he brings
A free first ways he brings
A received reach poverty mind he kept
Returning broken knees wizened tongues

Cut out eyes, sky alike made the spiritual wander the mountaintops
Moonlight futures rebellion.
Returning obscenity cunning in games
For laughter punched the producing upgrowth comfortable memories
To choices where your lone life livings together dip piled disgusted.
Outcast quiet surrounded birth
Sight those sadden ugly bushed pack blood making homes in
waterless waters.
Cast nightmare in day light schools injured clear-cut edged Woomera.
When fatally footprints powdered the every appearing so feared.
When devising success, a criminal to the carried spiritual coverings.
Swung thrower blend winds naked forming of energy to shape evil
helpless loves.
Upper twig cheek intention to contract,
'You kill all my kin to be lazy'
Greater joys in hallowed seeded plants
Breathing a reveal in sane weathered our sacred
Ashes ancestors water hens oh don't come to my funeral
if you do not go to these dead one's
now death wishing by her was silly having no meaning
so where the love they say they had lost found or spaced
to timeless motes in your only lone nest by everyone around yam
cringes peace
payed for by who to who, life is cared life is eyes ears feets

MINYUNGAI (WHEN) BUD'HERA

MOON SLIVER PEACE
DIRTY ORIGIN
HARVEST LINGO
1840 IS NO DIFFERENT
BAD BLOOD BREW
Modules dead plays song relivable
Hosted truly chances
No Ethernet cross-cultural warrior's encounters
Those bridging birds services need why knowledge.
Solution my our indigenous
Theory gap unique connection
Happens by experiences spiritual,
Taste where wealth participants.
International interfaces
Effective those struggles.
Awareness differences answers
Quester range death by suicidal thoughts.
Warriors strategies natives modern Murri reality
Bite-sized our age lines level
Together practical vacillator
Dirty modules dead playing songs encounters Warriors'
Gaps interfaces
Most are kum'bun.........
Most are gumeras......
Most are international poets left by the roadsides.
Where are those warriors foot on arms lone?
Where are those minds stands on your lands under fenced?

No internet brewing peace these days
Defect harvest gold blooded by experiences
Differ cross these rods origin high on slivers
Up jumps the Bi-ol (Fathers) happenings
Up jumps those Mothers unwanted for the connective lifers
Rile fall live sleep as if awakening to a voice's sound
Sat down now the so-called warriors
Stand down warriors cannot speak by the how much money
Tells the wealth more to the speakers written words.
Many lips run wet, your one an alone man...

Mr YARRY FO TUGAI BORROL WALLULI 'MANY'

Yaw IMABURRA MINYU DALLA
Pace run in our silence
She flies nature so wise
She morning birds aloud so
Our seeds meet flowers
Night autumn lifes to NYAMUL (young)
Unbait + Bright NYAMUL.
Where lit lights grow glare?
Dark trees leaves
A breeze air on cheated mans
Afternoon rest asleep for
WARRILL All 'Humans' awake to
Beautifully butterfly ants' dirt hole heats
GURUA a cold fog clear lost worlds
BOOERNER Up early
GITTI TAGI (Mountain)
DILLI (EYES) ARMS
Fingers to legs the feet at how old bodies
Age tells by the bodies.
BIBU TAGI MOUNTAIN GIVTH

Nature Herage Are All Ages

Fist finger small rivets rivers
    Logan + ILL – Bogan
Many water change colours not rained
We walking the creek bed rain drops
We feet all hairs under falling
    Stars morning bright
We sunshine arms passion eyes twine
As ripple image of an old tree BOORI
Ash shore felon by the enemy ray frazzle
Babe
Lilly papers spring from above a babe mountain.
Bogs logs taken ants' logs nature fallen
Dragon flying air along wings' breeze
Thrown fish high jumping
Birds awaking the rocked bottom
Rivers sand felted reefs bark dead spin leaves branches
On banks side month's ready
To swim sing dance winds
Blowing time spaces in to ward butterfly word words.
She fishes all the dip lip out
She wishes hall dear stop the dams
Relive her going fishing day
Nights alive
We fish a line, forgot blades
Yes, kainite fin fist hands behind
Blood no caught today lush rush
Luck another creek drain by

Dragnet road alike of fish
Nature herbage are all ages
Fist high small even big name poets
Logan City will never know

Palya Palya Dha

Ian Djani
Mundoi mundi mulla mulla
Whadajna gooly gooly
Gooncle goongal joonnoo jinang jambi
Paibun mogwi burri burri binjori burri burri
Binnai boonga gurri-goo
Gurdiga gurdiga
Buran buran
Dilli dilli doori doori
Doongi doongi gooncle
Goolahji goolahjie
Mookadook mookadook Moodaguardi
Whjbou yubba doongi dimbanjin dimbanjin
Palya palya mitti mitti djani djani
Dhagun dhagu

By Our Memories Zapata

No verse justice for peoples
Americanos Mexican Australian
Let peace drop PM knows the poets' mon,
Zapata Mexican year.
Where are these Australian Mexican ago?
No justice Zapata farmers are grained
By no justice, see 1919 same as 2019
Seeing E. MILIANO
Where are these mosaics Mexican Australians?
No verse a ride camel
Donkey horses.
Zap pet ta revisionary
Peace winds face eyes awaken before
Laws unjust ices to a justices.
We are these Mexican Australian
Let no peace be government member families
August 2018, 1879 rasping flags causes we'll
Stone your ideas down.
Non poets never revolutionary
Señor ZAPATA
VIVA

Acknowledgements

Thanks to Mia Tinkler and Alex Vella-Horne for their consistent support through edits and in helping with the preparations for this book.

And thanks to Ivor Indyk for having all the patience with me and for supporting me to get this book out.

About the author

Lionel G. Fogarty is a Yugambeh man, and was born on Wakka Wakka land in South Western Queensland near Murgon on a 'punishment reserve' outside Cherbourg. Throughout the 1970s, he worked as an activist for Aboriginal Land Rights and protesting Aboriginal deaths in custody. In 1993, his younger brother, Daniel Yock, died while in police custody. He has published numerous collections of poetry, including most recently the award-winning *Connection Requital; Mogwie-Idan: Stories of the Land;* and *Eelahroo (Long Ago) Nyah (Looking) Möbö-Möbö (Future),* and *Selected Poems 1980–2017.*